EI SECRETS

THE 30 DAY
EMOTIONAL INTELLIGENCE
EXPERIENCE

DB BEDFORD

EI Secrets: The 30 Day Emotional Intelligence Experience
Copyright © 2019 by Derrick DB Bedford
ALL RIGHTS RESERVED

ISBN - 9781075459092

Cover Design: Horseplay Studios/Stacey Debono
Edited by: Stacey Debono

PLEASE NOTE: This book complements the *30 Day EI Experience* online course. While this book can be used as a standalone challenge, we strongly encourage you to use this book alongside the online course for maximum value.

For more information, contact us at:
www.30dayeiexperience.com
db.bedford@ineverworry.com

 De'Morea Evans shared his first post.
✋ New Member · 1 hr · 🖼

I know I'm a day behind but I completed Day 1 yesterday. It's amazing how when you really want to do something and it's put on the front of your mind....how much you really pay attention to things. "WILLINGNESS" I think the Seat Belt to Success! No matter what the road SHOW...."WILLINGNESS" will help you to GO! And it helped me to pay more attention to what was around me and how I was handling myself in conversation or around people. Ready for day ✌️

Table of Contents

EI Secret #1: *Emotional Willingness* 7

EI Secret #2: *Stealth Mode Emotions* 13

EI Secret #3: *Control, ALT, Delete* 19

EI Secret #4: *Don't Bite the Hook* 25

EI Secret #5: *Emotional Maturity* 29

EI Secret #6: *Emotional Baggage* 33

EI Secret #7: *Emotional Grudges* 39

EI Secret #8: *Emotional Growth* 45

EI Secret #9: *Emotional Attachments* 49

EI Secret #10: *Emotional Confusion* 53

EI Secret #11: *Emotional Procrastination* 57

EI Secret #12: *Emotional Balance* 61

EI Secret #13: *Emotional Preparedness* 67

EI Secret #14: *Emotional Mathematics* 71

EI Secret #15: *Emotional Storyboard* 77

EI Secret #16: *Emotional Parenting* 83

EI Secret #17: *Emotional Vibrations* 89

EI Secret #18: *Emotional Biases* 95

EI Secret #19: *Emotional Patience* 101

EI Secret #20: *Taking Things Personally* 107

EI Secret #21: *The Emotional Beast* 113

EI Secret #22: *Behavior Detection* 119

EI Secret #23: *Emotional Distractions* 125

EI Secret #24: *Week One Recap* 129

EI Secret #25: *Week Two Recap* 135

EI Secret #26: *Week Three Recap* 141

EI Secret #27: *Emotional Attitude* 147

EI Secret #28: *What is Your Why?* 153

EI Secret #29: *Emotional Acceptance* 159

EI Secret #30: *Congrats!* 163

About the Author 169

EI Secret #1: *Emotional Willingness*

Welcome to Day One of your EI Challenge!

I take my hat off to you for taking this challenge because we all really need to be honest about the impact emotions have on our day-to-day lives. Emotionally charged situations can show up in our lives very quickly, and if you're not viewing your life through the lens of Emotional Intelligence, you're going to get caught off guard every single time. The things that you say and do, and how you react when something is emotionally charged, can be very sensitive in nature and we can find ourselves in a space where we have to come back and redo some restorative justice or damage control.

A wise man once said, "He who flies off in a rage never has a safe landing." When you pop off about something because you are emotionally charged or act rashly in reaction to something that someone said to you, and you start telling yourself a story about why there's been some injustice done to you, it's going to disrupt your energy every single time. Your focus is going to be taken from your peace in that moment. This 30 Day Challenge is designed to minimize those low frequency situations and ensure successful communication and relationships on all levels and every situation.

Of course, it's not always going to be easy and there are going to be times where you may miss the mark but if you are committed to this Emotional Intelligence platform, you will begin to recognize how to bounce back quickly and effectively and stay on track. The harder we fall, the higher we bounce back, and the more you feel empowered to resolve those tough situations through the lens of Emotional Intelligence, the stronger and more successful you're going to be. The people around you are going to start to notice it as well, and they're going to be craving that knowledge you possess. You're going to become a credible messenger of peace in your social circle because Emotional Intelligence is contagious.

You have just made one of the best decisions of your life to begin living your life through the lens of Emotional Intelligence. This is how it works: every day you should strive to read a chapter that reveals a new EI secret, then focus on that secret for the following twenty-four hours. Consciously think about that secret: write it down, put it into the notepad in your cell phone, make it a screenshot and read it throughout the day, whatever you need to do, just consciously and deeply think about that secret of the day. Stay focused every day and be true and honest with yourself with the questions at the end of the chapters, too. This is for *your* benefit, and a gift you're giving yourself. At the same time, don't worry if you miss a day or two. It's easy to jump back in and get back on track.

Before we get started, we have to lay the foundation. Your first EI secret today is going to be about your **emotional willingness**. Are you willing to become emotionally intelligent? That might sound a little crazy because you may be thinking, "Hey DB, I'm here. What do you mean 'am I willing'?" Well, there are a lot of things that we *do*. We join the gym, but we might not follow through and go. We start diets, but we might not follow through and stay with them. We open books, but we may not follow through and read them. A lot of our success, or lack thereof, has to do with our willingness *to follow through*.

Challenge your emotional willingness in the next twenty-four hours. Think about how willing you are to exercise your Emotional Intelligence in potentially uncomfortable conversations when you need it the most. One of the most common things I see is that people are fine when everything is going well but when things don't go our way, what do we do? We resist. You have to be willing to follow through when it's the toughest; when your wife, your husband, your kids, or that coworker gets on your last nerve. Will you use Emotional Intelligence to deal with those tough situations? Make sure to look for these types of situations in the next twenty-four hours or think about a situation that didn't go so well where you could have used Emotional Intelligence and ask yourself, "Would I have been willing in that moment?"

CHALLENGE - DAY 1
EMOTIONAL WILLINGNESS

Challenge your emotional willingness. For the next twenty-four hours, pay attention to the things that may rub you the wrong way. Pay attention to what is happening around you, to how you feel about those things, and to those moments where you might have said, "I don't want to hear that Emotional Intelligence stuff right now."

Are you emotionally willing right now? _____

What has rubbed you the wrong way recently, and how did you feel about it?

_____
_____
_____
_____
_____
_____
_____
_____
_____
_____

What situation(s) arose *recently* in which you could have used Emotional Intelligence?

_____
_____
_____
_____
_____

What situation(s) have come up in the *past* that could have benefited from the use of Emotional Intelligence?

_____
_____
_____
_____
_____
_____
_____
_____
_____

How does using Emotional Intelligence neutralize negative situations?

_____
_____
_____
_____
_____
_____
_____
_____

_____
_____
_____
_____
_____
_____
_____
_____
_____
_____
_____
_____
_____
_____
_____
_____
_____
_____
_____
_____
_____
_____
_____
_____
_____
_____
_____
_____
_____
_____

EI Secret #2: *Stealth Mode Emotions*

Today's challenge is something that can be very difficult to detect when it comes to Emotional Intelligence. It really drives the way people feel about you and drives the way you feel about things. One of the things that I always talk about is how what is not measured cannot be managed. If you can't measure something, if you can't identify something, then you can't manage it.

Has someone ever been upset or frustrated with you about something that you've done or said, but they didn't tell you? Usually when this happens, there's conversation that's happening around the incident that you know nothing about – the person that is upset might be talking to everyone else but you about what is bothering them. You're just going on about your business, and you have no idea you've offended them.

These are called **stealth mode emotions,** meaning the emotions are so hidden and undetected that you didn't even know they existed. People are upset with or bothered by you, but they don't tell you there is a problem. They talk to you, they have had numerous opportunities to share with you how they feel, yet they choose not to – they are in stealth mode with their emotions.

There are one of two ways you may uncover how they feel. One, they tell somebody else who tells you, or two, you realize that the energy between you and this person has changed. If you are astute to Emotional Intelligence, depending on where you are with it, your situational awareness might kick in. You might feel these vibes and ask the person about it. They may not be honest about it the first time you ask and may deny that anything is wrong so you have to ask again, and then they might finally tell you.

This may have even been you once or twice. There may be things that you have felt a certain way about and you didn't address the situation with the person who may have offended you. Unidentified emotions can never be managed, and many people don't even realize that this is what they're doing.

When you're looking at the world through the lens of Emotional Intelligence, you will be able to pay attention to shifts in energy because your energy and other people's energy will introduce them as they step into the room, before they even say anything. You will recognize that there is a problem, address it in an appropriate manner, and get on with your day.

We are just warming up, so be aware of these secrets and internalize them. The first domain in Emotional Intelligence is self-awareness. Once you're aware, you'll be able to manage your reactions, which is the second domain in Emotional Intelligence. Situational awareness will help you understand which energies you need to connect to in every situation, and which energies you need to stay away from. When you have all these things going on, you can better manage your relationships.

Understanding these secrets keeps you conscious of Emotional Intelligence at all times and after some conscious practice, it will become second nature. Getting up every single day and looking at the world through the lens of Emotional Intelligence puts you at a higher frequency than most people you may encounter throughout the day, which keeps you focused and at peace.

 Daija Stafford
14 mins ·

Day 2, ive definitely been holding some stealth emotions towards some friends because I feel like they are doing the same thing, so I am going to express my thoughts to them in a conversational way to ensure it doesn't continue to happen

CHALLENGE – DAY 2
STEALTH MODE EMOTIONS

Now that you are aware of stealth mode emotions, spend the next twenty-four hours thinking about those times when you may have been upset or bothered by someone and you didn't address the situation. Additionally, pay attention to anyone who may be in stealth mode around you. Has there been a change in energy in anyone around you at work, home or socially?

Are you in stealth mode right now? If so, are you willing to have an emotionally intelligent conversation with them to clear the air?

_____
_____
_____
_____
_____
_____
_____
_____

How did being in stealth mode in the past affect that relationship?

_____
_____
_____
_____
_____
_____
_____

Is anybody around you in stealth mode? Have you asked them about what might be bothering them?

_____

_____

_____

_____

_____

_____

_____

_____

EI Secret #3: *Control, ALT, Delete*

Today's secret is about a strategy that you can use at a moment's notice when you encounter a little turbulence in your day. It's really about resetting and reconnecting to a positive space when situations seem to pop up out of nowhere.

This is one of my all-time favorites because it's pretty simple and direct. I like to call it a secret because when people hear it, they light up because it's a familiar phrase. If your computer is stuck or is responding slowly, there's a method that we utilize to fix that, or at least try to, and that's hitting the *control, alt, and delete* buttons. When you hit these buttons, we are essentially resetting things to get our computer going again or getting the option to reboot.

When it comes to Emotional Intelligence, I want you to practice that same methodology. *Control* your emotions in any situation. *ALT*, always search for alternate solutions to negative situations. *Delete* all the toxic connections to whatever it is that's happening. *Control, ALT, Delete.*

If a situation arises where something isn't vibrating the way you want it to, whatever it is, step back for a minute and think to yourself: *Control*, I need to control myself in this moment. *Alt*, what is the alternative? What else can I be doing in this situation? *Delete*, let me disconnect, let me delete, let me get rid of that bad energy so I don't have to deal with it anymore. In situations like this, especially the ones that are weighing heavy on you, this is one secret you can't afford to be without.

If you are practicing these secrets, you are moving towards successfully practicing the Emotional Intelligence platform. Being emotionally intelligent is knowing and being aware of these secrets, utilizing them, being able to identify when it's a good time to use them, identifying when other people should be using them, and paying attention to the results. Being aware of them at all times is how you're going to get yourself to the EI space. You should be feeling a little bit more empowered by now. If you're talking about it, if you are really testing what I'm saying in "the real world", you'll see why these secrets are powerful; they're simple and they're effective. Even if you only remember one secret at the end of the thirty days, you're still going to move into the space of being emotionally intelligent because you're going to be that much more aware.

Let's keep on pushing, we're going to get through this. You're doing well! Hang in there.

CHALLENGE – DAY 3
Control, ALT, Delete

In the next twenty-four hours, think about a turbulent situation when Control, ALT, Delete could have helped. Throughout the day, be cognizant of these types of situations and think about Control, ALT, Delete: *Control*, take control of yourself. *Alt*, what is the alternative? What else can you be doing in this situation? *Delete*, delete any bad energy so you don't have to deal with it anymore.

In what positive ways could you control your emotions in an emotionally charged situation?

_____
_____
_____
_____
_____
_____
_____
_____

What might be some positive alternative solutions to negative situations?

_____
_____
_____
_____
_____
_____
_____
_____

How might you delete a toxic connection?

_____

_____

_____

_____

_____

Additional Thoughts on Control, ALT, Delete

_____

_____

_____

_____

_____

_____

_____

_____

_____

_____

_____

_____

_____

_____

_____

_____

_____

_____

_____

_____

_____

_____

_____

_____

_____

_____

_____

_____

_____

_____

_____

EI Secret #4: *Don't Bite the Hook*

Today's challenge is one that I think will definitely become very obvious in your everyday life once you get the hang of it. You will feel better about yourself for avoiding these pitfalls, too.

Imagine a happy little fish is swimming in the stream minding his own business, then the fish gets distracted by something shiny dangling in the water, a big sharp hook. He goes for it, bites the hook and ends up getting snatched out of his environment, never to return to his peaceful little stream again. This EI secret is called, "**Don't Bite the Hook.**"

On a day to day basis, there are a lot of hooks out there waiting to bait you and if you bite them, you will be just like that fish. You will get snatched out of your peace and you're going to be taken in a whole new direction. You're going to be distracted and taken out of your peaceful little stream. For example, biting the hook can happen when somebody is rude or discourteous to you. By responding and matching their energy with negativity, you just bit the hook and now you're engaging in conflict. You could be tempted to bite the hook while you're driving and someone cuts you off, drives too slowly, or takes too long at the light, and you may find yourself beginning to engage in a negative interaction with them. All of these situations are going to slow you down from getting to where you need to be. The negative energy may not end in that moment either. It can have lasting effects and may linger for hours, days, or longer with potentially serious life altering consequences.

Negative conversations are potential hooks as well. We may have friends and family that call and lower our vibration with negative or depressing conversations. If you engage in those conversations, you just bit the hook. If you start to believe that things are never going to be right for you, if you start to believe that your financial situation is never going to change for the better, that you're always going to have a low credit score or a poor living condition, and you never do anything to change your circumstances, you just bit the hook! I'm a strong believer in the laws of attraction in the universe. Whatever you put out is what you're going to get back.

Learn to identify, recognize, and then vibrate higher. That is a code, an EI secret that can help you stay in a positive space more often than not because there are hooks all throughout the day just waiting to snag you out of your peaceful stream. Looking at the world through this lens of Emotional Intelligence is going to help you avoid these distracting hooks by allowing you to identify them so you can avoid them, then you can go in a different direction and vibrate higher. An old wise man once said if you stop at every barking dog, you will never get to your destination. If you respond to every little thing that comes your way, you're going to be sidetracked from the important things. Life is way too short for all that.

CHALLENGE – DAY 4
DON'T BITE THE HOOK

Today is really about paying attention to those things that can take you off your path of growth, so for the next twenty-four hours, focus on not biting the hook. Pay attention to the subtle things that might draw you in and sidetrack you from whatever it is that you're trying to do. No exceptions. Pay attention to when someone is trying to lower your frequency and pull you into a negative situation or conversation. We all know the difference between positive and negative, so if it feels like it's negative, no matter who it is, *don't bite the hook*.

Thinking about the last twenty-four hours, list a few instances when you noticed a hook. What did you do?

_____
_____
_____
_____
_____
_____
_____
_____
_____

How might you avoid these hooks?

_____
_____
_____
_____
_____
_____
_____

El Secret #5: *Emotional Maturity*

Today I want to talk about **emotional maturity**. We talk about maturity a lot, and many people believe that because they are grown or have reached a certain age, they are mature. This is not necessarily true because maturity has a lot to do with life experiences. When we are young, most of us just haven't experienced enough to be fully mature.

Conversely, many adults find out, much to their surprise, that older adults are not as mature as they should be. Wisdom is acquired knowledge gained from life experiences, yet some people lack emotional maturity, even adults in their 40s, 50s, and 60s. When you look at someone who you feel should be exhibiting emotional maturity because of their age who then behaves a certain way or reacts in a very immature way, you may be very surprised at their lack of emotional maturity. Unfortunately, emotional maturity is not a given, at any age.

What is emotional maturity? It's when you understand that your emotions cannot be the driver of your decisions. When you are in a high emotional state, chances are you're going to make a decision that would be different had you stopped and thought rationally. But the real underlying key to emotional maturity (and this is the secret right here) is that you become unattached to being *right*. Let that sink in for a second. *You become unattached to being right*. You simply lose the desire to be right. This strategy alone will help you free yourself from a lot of emotional baggage.

One of the key elements of emotional maturity I've personally strived to master is my lack of desire to be right. Once I realize, while I'm having a discussion with someone, that we're not seeing eye to eye and they are set on what it is they believe, I'm okay with that. And here's the maturity part: I'm not mad at them for needing to be right, and I don't think any less of them. I don't have anything negative to say to them or about them. That's emotional maturity.

Many people become stressed out and frustrated, and relationships become strained simply because somebody is trying to be in the right. But at the end of the day, who cares? If I tell you that the best way to get somewhere is in a particular direction based on my experience and you think that another way is the way to go, that's fine. If I tell you something that I believe to be right, but you see it differently, that's ok too. When you understand perspective, you understand that two people can look at the same thing and each of them can see two different things.

 Carolyn V. Webb
★ Rising Star · 32 mins · 🆔

PSA I'd like to introduce EI/I Never Worry 30 day challenge to you. The challenge offers daily secret skills to control your emotions, enhance your people skills so you can operate in your better self! The challenge offers personal and corporate development skils needed to maneuver through your day. Sign up for the challenge watch your personal transformation!

CHALLENGE – DAY 5
EMOTIONAL MATURITY

Emotional maturity is the challenge for the day. Identify any areas in your life where you might feel like you may be overreacting to the little things, where you're not viewing things through the lens of Emotional Intelligence. For the next twenty-four hours, think about emotional maturity. Pay attention to situations and start the process of not having the desire to be right. This doesn't mean you're wrong! It just means you're not right to the other person or the situation.

Was there a situation today where you had to be right? Could you have let it go and just accepted someone else's perspective?

_____
_____
_____
_____
_____
_____
_____
_____
_____

How does not having the desire the be right play into Emotional Intelligence?

_____
_____
_____
_____
_____
_____
_____

EI Secret #6: *Emotional Baggage*

Today's secret is going to further you in the quest to becoming emotionally intelligent. First, let me tell you about a situation that happened to me.

I was on the phone with a buddy of mine and while we were talking, another phone call came in from a number that I struggle with every time I see it, and always wonder whether or not I should answer. I have a family member who is in prison, and he's going to be there for the rest of his life. He's been there for several years now and the whole time he's been in there, I've been trying to explain to him in the most respectful way possible that I am not in a position to take care of him financially. I have a lot of responsibilities and besides that, I don't necessarily agree with what he did to land him in prison.

However, the human side of me has made it a point to look out for him from time to time, even though I said that I wouldn't. He keeps coming back and asking for things and I feel a certain kind of way about that. When he can't reach me, he'll give someone else my number and have them call me to ask me for things for him. That rubs me the wrong way because not only am I really not that comfortable with continually having this conversation

33

with him, I really don't like that he's given someone else my number.

So now I'm on the phone with my buddy and we're talking business and this familiar number comes up, and I send it directly to voicemail. But now it's disrupted my entire thought process and our whole conversation. I explained the situation to him, and he completely related because he, too, has a family member incarcerated who does the same thing. We ended up having a conversation about people in custody, but now the whole conversation is derailed. This made me realize that I really needed to dismiss that number and never look back.

At the same time I was having this conversation, I happened to notice an email notification on my phone. The email said, "I just called you. Please call me back when you can." It was a potential client. Had I not seen that email right then and there, I could've missed an opportunity to get more business because I was in my feelings about my family member. The minute I saw that number come up, I got emotionally charged and I dismissed everything else.

I called the potential client right back, secured the deal, and put another paying gig on the books.

The EI secret for today is about **emotional baggage**. We have to be careful of the emotional baggage that we carry. I've been carrying this baggage around about how I feel about my family member and that baggage disrupted a conversation I was having in the present, and I might have even missed an opportunity to get more business on the books.

Here's another way to think about it: it's not just about me giving him a couple of hundred dollars, there's so much more involved. Yes, my family member is in jail, but I didn't have anything to do with that. It was lowering my vibration. I need to free myself from that emotional baggage; I need to unpack it and unburden myself.

The Emotional Intelligence platform has four quadrants. Self-awareness, managing your reactions, situational awareness, and managing relationships. The way that I should be managing this relationship is to confront my family member with the inevitable conversation. I need to tell him, "Listen. I am going to say this to you one last time. I will no longer take care of you." I have identified the baggage, and I'm unpacking it. It's not always easy, but very beneficial in the long run.

The EI secret of emotional baggage ties into the EI domain of managing relationships, and the sub-text is to have those necessary conversations. If there's a conversation we need to have with somebody to free us from that baggage, we need to do it without delay. Any time you're feeling a certain kind of way about something and you're carrying it around with you, consider it emotional baggage and know that you need to unpack it. The sooner, the better.

Have you ever carried luggage around when you went on a trip? One bag might be okay for a short distance. But what about two bags? It starts to weigh you down. When you carry three bags you're really starting to feel weighed down. The heavier it gets, the more it slows you down. The longer you hold on to it, the heavier it can feel, too. If it slows you down, it keeps you from getting to the space where you need to be. It's the same thing with this emotional baggage.

If your emotional baggage is weighing you down, then it keeps you from being open to your clarity, to your opportunities, and from optimizing your performance on a day to day basis so you can be the best version of yourself.

CHALLENGE – DAY 6
EMOTIONAL BAGGAGE

Your challenge for today is to unpack any emotional baggage that you may have; have those necessary conversations, if possible. If the luggage is too heavy, just start the process of unpacking it by embracing your feelings, processing them and leveraging them to create the best possible outcome based on the situation. Be mindful of the emotional baggage that you carry. Once you identify it, you will find that you *want* to unpack it and unburden yourself. Why? Because it's heavy, and it's an emotional burden.

What steps did you take today to unpack your emotional baggage?

_____
_____
_____
_____
_____
_____
_____
_____

How did it feel once you took those steps?

_____
_____
_____
_____
_____
_____
_____

Additional Thoughts on Emotional Baggage

_____

_____

_____

_____

_____

_____

_____

_____

_____

_____

_____

_____

_____

_____

_____

_____

_____

_____

_____

_____

_____

_____

_____

_____

_____

_____

_____

_____

_____

_____

EI Secret #7: *Emotional Grudges*

Today's secret really complements yesterday's secret about emotional baggage so if you did your homework your goal was to take a look at your emotional baggage and the things you are carrying with you and recognize that you have the ability to unpack all of that to unburden yourself.

There is baggage that we all have been carrying since early childhood; traumas and life experiences we may not have yet unpacked and do not realize how it is affecting our level of clarity. The purpose of being emotionally intelligent is one, so that you can protect your peace at all times; and two, so that you are able to operate on a higher frequency and optimize your performance every single day no matter what it is that you do.

Today's secret is about **emotional grudges**. It really goes hand in hand with baggage. These grudges are emotions held toward other people for things that they did or didn't do for you. Do you hold any grudges right now? Is there somebody that you do not like that you refuse to talk to or interact with because of some negative interaction you had in the past? If so, you may be holding a grudge.

The thing about grudges is that there's such a disadvantage to the person who's holding them. Nine times out of ten, the other person has moved on, or the situation has long passed. An old wise man once said that holding a grudge or resentment is like taking poison and expecting the other person to die.

You have to free yourself and let things go. Why? Because it truly doesn't matter in the grand scheme of things, and the more you hold on, the heavier the weight is for you to carry.

Remember those four domains of Emotional Intelligence: *self-awareness, managing reactions, situational awareness, and managing relationships.* You cannot manage a relationship effectively when you're holding a grudge. Communicate to that person if they did something to you that you feel was wrong at the appropriate time. Release that grudge so that you can begin to unpack that baggage.

I like to say the best time to have a bad conversation is when something is going well, and the best time to have a good conversation is when things are not going so well. When you articulate your emotions when it's not an emotionally charged situation, a person is more likely to be open to hearing what is on your mind and resolve the situation positively.

There are people I don't necessarily care for; we all have them, but I'm not holding a grudge against them. There are people who have deliberately tried to take away my livelihood, tried to slander my name. I'm okay with that. I don't hold a grudge against them because I understand that everybody has their own perspective and not everyone has to like me.

Oftentimes, we get upset if we hear someone "doesn't like us." And what's the first thing we do? We might automatically react from the hip with, "Well, I don't like them either!" But why? You may not even know them, or perhaps they didn't even do anything to you. They decided, for whatever reason, they just don't like you.

But here's the thing. You've got to show love even when they don't, or you just become one of them. The whole thing about living this life is not about being soft, and it's not about being stepped on. There's a time to be firm, and we're going to talk about that too, but there's a time where you have to give in a bit to protect your peace.

Emotional Intelligence is not about telling you how to feel. You need to be able to step back after you have said what you need to. Disconnect the emotion so you can reconnect and either resolve that situation or determine that there will be no further communication; but be free about it. That's the key.

If you can get a handle on your emotional grudges along with your emotional baggage, you are another step closer to being emotionally intelligent. All of these different ideologies are time tested through the practice of looking at the world through the lens of Emotional Intelligence. That's why everything has an emotional pretext to it, because as emotionally intelligent beings we need to look at the world this way.

Shannon Pdc Owens
8 mins ·

Emotional Baggage & Grudges.... hmm... I must say I recognized this in my two millennial daughters. No matter what is going on if I think everything is all good some how in some way they remind me of how bad their childhood was and how messed up I was. Now, during these times I now know that I have to exercise my emotional maturity because I instantly want to defend myself, but in reality they are entitled to their opinions and honestly half the stuff I don't even remember. I will start acknowledging their feelings and apologizing even for stuff I don't remember because my peace is precious to me & I want them to have some resolution as well. I love reminiscing about the past and talking about the fun times where we all end up laughing so unpacking my baggage and letting go of grudges (tbh yes, I have held grudges against my children when they make me the bad guy even though I was a single mom, working a manual job, going to school, and raised them in the process), but what I am learning is that grudges is for suckas.... don't want to be a sucka no more... in my Joe voice...😂😂 #lovingthis30dayEIchallenge

CHALLENGE – DAY 7
EMOTIONAL GRUDGES

For the next twenty-four hours, if you have a grudge - and think hard before you say you don't have any grudges! - *let them go.* How do you let them go? Like Nike, just do it. Remove the personal feelings you have about whatever happened and take into consideration that you don't know the whole story or why people act the way that they do. If those two things are not motivation enough, know that you're in this challenge and you're moving to the space of being an emotionally intelligent person, and those of us who operate in this space just don't hold grudges.

Now you have a couple of reasons to give yourself the value of letting these grudges go. Take the next twenty-four hours to do just that.

Think about the instances where you have grudges and consciously tell yourself "I will let it go." How does this make you feel?

_____

_____

_____

_____

_____

How can you avoid holding grudges in the future?

_____

_____

_____

_____

_____

EI Secret #8: *Emotional Growth*

Today we're going to talk about **emotional growth**. Because you're here and taking this challenge, it's apparent that you are interested in growing. By nature, humans want to grow. We grow physically whether we want to or not, but we also like to grow spiritually, we like to mature, we like to succeed. Sometimes we don't always get there.

Say your goal is to get stronger or lose weight, but you don't feel like going to the gym or you don't feel like changing your eating habits. Say you want to make more money, but you don't feel like getting an actual job, or you don't feel like creating your own business. How do you reach the level of success that you're looking for? How do you actually get it done? Well, the answer is one of the many secrets in Emotional Intelligence, so I'm going to provide you with a life hack to push through those emotional moments when you're trying to grow and find yourself running into barriers.

A good life hack is to adopt the 1% rule, which means that you will improve yourself by just 1% every single day. That's probably the minimal effort you can give to something; but if you put your focus on one thing, whatever it is in your life you're trying to do, and you go at it 1% daily, in one year's time you'll be 365% better in any area in your life.

My goal is to read more but I feel like I don't have time to read and can't sit still for too long. I use the 1% rule and all I have to do is just pick up a book and read maybe one page a day. If the book is really large, all I have to commit to is maybe ten pages. Whatever the math works out to be for the number of pages in the book, I just make my goal 1% of the book every day.

If you need to drink more water, start with drinking one glass or even half a glass, just 1% more than what you're actually drinking now. If you want to stop drinking alcohol, then stop drinking by 1% every single day. Over a period of time, you can stop drinking completely. Any habits you want to change, any goal you want to accomplish, you go at it 1% at a time. The theory behind this is that anything that you do in increments of 1% should be an easy win. Once you get an easy win, you will feel good about that win which will encourage you to go at it again tomorrow.

Don't be afraid to challenge yourself! You're going to feel better about your accomplishments within a short period of time. We all know when you feel better, you do better. Small steps will get you to the bigger picture. Slow motion is still motion.

CHALLENGE – DAY 8
EMOTIONAL GROWTH

For the next twenty-four hours, identify what it is that you need to improve on in your life and do 1% towards that goal. Focus on one thing that you need to challenge.

What do you feel you need to improve on in your life that you could change by just 1% today?

_____

_____

_____

_____

_____

_____

_____

_____

_____

How will you go about making that change?

_____

_____

_____

_____

_____

_____

_____

_____

_____

EI Secret #9: *Emotional Attachments*

Hopefully by now you're starting to get into the rhythm of each secret and taking the time to really think about them and applying them to your daily routines because that's the key. It's one thing to learn something, but quite another to apply it to your daily life. Additionally, taking the time to answer the questions at the end of each chapter. Thinking about how these secrets apply to you can really go a long way in making Emotional Intelligence second nature.

Studies show that if we do something consecutively for at least 28 days, it increases the chances of it becoming a habit, and the habit I want you to create is to look at things through the lens of Emotional Intelligence. Today's secret is very powerful because so many people have these without even realizing they have them. Today's secret is *emotional attachments.* Every day it seems that at some point we find ourselves experiencing what I like to call the "I have to do this" syndrome. "I have to do this, I have to do that." "I can't do this, because I have to do that." It can happen in a conversation where somebody says something to you, or does something to you, or does something that you don't like, and you feel like you have to respond. You know you should be doing something to take care of yourself, but you say, "I can't, because I have to do that."

This is because you have an emotional attachment to the "I have to do." If you can be mindful of the things that you emotionally attach yourself to, then you can move into a more peaceful space. When you emotionally attach yourself to the "I have to do this," "I have to be over here," "I have to get this done," "I can't do this because I have to do that," etc., you find yourself all over the place. That does not help you operate in an emotionally intelligent space because you're always being pulled in different directions. See where I'm going with that? If you're always being pulled in different directions, it's hard to operate in peace.

I like to use this analogy: if you are always emotionally attached to things and you're stuck in this *I have to do this, I have to do that* mode, then it's like you're the TV in life and every other thing has the remote control. Life is pushing the buttons and controlling what channel you're on, and that's not the way to be.

 Xiomara Linda Guerrero ▶ **Emotional Intelligence for Women**
3 hrs ·

I am so grateful for the 30 day challenge. Today I know I used all of the secrets. As a result I am confident in were I said with this one girl who is trying hard to knock me off my square. Not going to happen I am emotionally intelligent today. Thank DB.

CHALLENGE – DAY 9
EMOTIONAL ATTACHMENTS

Take the next twenty-four hours and pay attention to the things to which you are emotionally attached, as well as observe some things other people may be emotionally attached to and reflect on them.

What are some material things to which you are emotionally attached?

_____
_____
_____
_____
_____
_____
_____
_____
_____
_____
_____

What are some things that you have noticed that others may be emotionally attached to, and how does this affect their Emotional Intelligence?

_____
_____
_____
_____
_____
_____
_____
_____

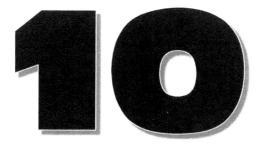

EI Secret #10: *Emotional Confusion*

Welcome to Day 10!

Recently I was planning to get an alarm service installed at my house and during the process a lot of things were not in alignment. The alarm company's deliverables were not what they said they were going to be. Different people in the organization had different perspectives of what should be and shouldn't be taking place and no one could give me a clear idea on price and the exact services they offered. It was frustrating and confusing. I looked on the website, I called the sales department, I called management and finally I gave up and cancelled the service.

This whole situation made me think about today's secret, **emotional confusion.** Because of this situation, emotional confusion became clear to me. In marketing, they say that a confused mind will almost always say "no." Think about when you may have been confused about something. If something isn't clear or you're uncertain, there is a certain level of emotion attached to it. The emotion that usually comes with it is frustration simply because you may not understand the situation. This tends to create an emotional connection to anger, the cousin to frustration. You may get angry about the situation, which may ultimately lead to a rash decision which will need damage control later.

Take a look at the things in your life that you might be confused about. Perhaps it's a relationship, your finances, maybe even a tough decision that you're struggling with. Pay attention to the confusion that's attached to it, because when you neutralize the confusion you will have more clarity to make the right decision. If, however, you try to make a decision in the midst of confusion, you will probably make an abrupt choice, much like the one I made about the alarm system. It was based on frustration and not on Emotional Intelligence.

If the alarm company sales rep had taken the time to make sure that everything was very clear and was more knowledgeable about the company's products, then the deal would have gone through. Instead, I had to decide while I was confused, and the result was an unhappy customer; I am not getting the system I wanted. I have to restart the entire process and go through it all again, and that has an emotion attached to it, too, because my entire day was disrupted.

The minute you are uncertain, or you're confused about something, take a time out. Think to yourself, "Okay, so that I don't operate in this emotional confusion, let me seek some clarity as quickly as possible; and if I have to, I will just disconnect to reconnect." You don't want to make a decision while you're in that state of emotional confusion.

CHALLENGE – DAY 10
EMOTIONAL CONFUSION

For the next twenty-four hours pay attention to anything that you're confused about in your life, right now in the present or perhaps something you've been confused about in the past. Rethink that connection, and how it felt.

What decision did you make, and what was the outcome of that decision?

_____
_____
_____
_____
_____
_____
_____
_____
_____
_____
_____
_____

What could you have done to prevent rash decisions from being made while confused?

_____
_____
_____
_____
_____
_____
_____
_____
_____
_____
_____

El Secret #11: *Emotional Procrastination*

I am so excited that you are embracing what's being shared with you, and I know by now you've had some "Aha!" moments. It's very hard not to have that experience, because all of these secrets speak to things we experience every day. If you have not yet experienced how powerful Emotional Intelligence is, or least how powerful the secrets are, then I would challenge you to rethink your beliefs about the whole process. Think about your emotional willingness, and about challenging your own beliefs about Emotional Intelligence. A lot of times our beliefs are what slow us down in getting things done.

Today's secret is associated with what slows us down, but it's also something I think that we all have done on occasion: **emotional procrastination**. Everybody knows about procrastination, we put off doing some things, or just outright haven't done them and made an excuse. You might not have thought about it being attached to emotions. Let's unpack that and think about it for a minute.

Let's say you made a new goal to start working out, or to eat healthier. When you don't reach that goal, what words have you said to yourself? The alarm goes off early Monday morning. As you hit the snooze button, you might think, "I'm too tired, I don't feel like going to the gym this morning. I'll start tomorrow." When you did not stick to your healthy eating plan, and instead stopped at a fast food restaurant, you may have thought, "I'm in a hurry, I don't feel like taking the time to shop for something healthy today. I'll do it later." It's the same thing with finances and money when you want to save for something later but put it off. As the saying goes, tomorrow never comes.

How do we correct this? It starts with being honest about the way you feel about your goal, and then do it anyway. Remember, Emotional Intelligence has two parts: *emotion*, how you feel about something and *intelligence*, what you do with that feeling.

How do you counter that component of "How do I feel?" or more specifically, those feelings of "I don't feel like getting up and working out this morning" or "I don't feel like sticking to my healthy eating plan today"? What do you do with those feelings? Acknowledge them, embrace them, then proceed on to your goal. Do not allow those feelings to dictate your direction and take you off your path. It's like when you feel like saying the wrong thing to someone. Some lady just criticized your outfit, and you want to tell that person that she's a mean old clown, but you don't. Your Emotional Intelligence keeps you from doing it because you know that's not the smartest way to respond. You subconsciously acknowledge this thought and dismiss it, then proceed on with your day. Emotional Intelligence!

When you wake up every day, after you acknowledge whatever higher being you respect or whatever it is that you do when you first get up, say to yourself, "I'm stepping into the world today with my EI lens on!" then proceed accordingly with the secrets you've learned so far.

58

CHALLENGE – DAY 11
EMOTIONAL PROCRASTINATION

Think about some things that you've procrastinated about recently, perhaps some things that you're procrastinating about right now.

What are you procrastinating about right now? What about some things you might have procrastinated about in the past? What emotions are attached to that procrastination?

_____
_____
_____
_____
_____
_____
_____
_____

How does procrastination hinder Emotional Intelligence?

_____
_____
_____
_____
_____
_____
_____
_____
_____
_____
_____
_____

EI Secret #12: *Emotional Balance*

Today's secret is one that will level the playing field for all of these secrets, so I'll jump right in. This one is about **emotional balance**. Emotional Intelligence has never been about telling anybody how to feel. That just wouldn't make any sense. We want to be conscious, but we can't really control what runs up on us every day.

Some of you might be in a situation where you have a lot of toxic stuff going on every single day, but you haven't been able to see the light yet; or you might be having a lot of good stuff going on, and you haven't felt the dark yet. The key to Emotional Intelligence is having emotional balance.

My daughter was telling my wife and I the other day about something she learned in school and I thought it was pretty prolific. She told us how a lot of the time we cause our own stress, and when things are not what we expect them to be, our brain starts trying to figure out what's next. Her example was that if I were to hand you a pear and tell you it tasted like an apple, your mind is going to fight with you and tell you that there's no way this pear could taste like an apple because it's a pear, even though it's quite possible it could taste like an apple. Your brain will get stuck on the idea that there is no way a pear can taste like an apple.

In my journey to becoming a vegetarian, things like eggplant and tofu were not on my list of things that I even wanted to try, so the first thing I would say when I came across them was, "I don't want that. I don't like them." But the reality of it is, how did I even know I didn't like them? I'd never even tried them! There have been green veggie drinks I've seen at Trader Joe's and I've automatically said, "I'm not going to like that." Then I tried them and loved them.

What does that all have to do with emotions and balance? My daughter explained that when you come to a scenario where your brain is challenging the validity of what you're seeing, it's time to "open up a new file" just like on your computer. You organize your files into folders and when you want to organize something new, what do you do? You open a new file. If you try to put business documents in your vacation pictures folder, it's not going to make sense. When you want to go back to find it you may even forget you put it there, and it's going to be a struggle.

Opening a new file in your mind is just a way of opening a new perspective. I've always said that it's hard to see the picture when you're sitting inside the frame. Be open to new possibilities, whether it's someone else's perspective, a new work assignment, new foods, or new experiences.

I'm not one who likes to put things together with my hands such as furniture, but the few times that I've had to do it, I end up doing it incorrectly. Now, when I have to do this task, I open a new file and tell myself, "I got this." My last win was putting together an exercise bike. I had actually paid someone to assemble it for me, but that never happened, so when I got the bike I looked at it and thought, "I ought to be able to do this." I slowed my thought processes down, opened a new file, read the instructions, and took my time. I actually got it done, and correctly!

Emotional balance is taking everything in and compartmentalizing in a way that doesn't weigh too heavy one way or another. That's the key. Keep that balance, because whether you're having a good day or a bad day, it is the only day that you have.

Jas Lee ▶ **iNeverWorry Academy**
20 mins · 🖼

Just wanted to give a huge shout out to **Db Bedford** thank you for being you and all you do! You're like the uncle of EI! The 30 day challenge is helping me alot! It was a great feeling being in family court yesterday and not getting emotional at all.. Still being able to be persistent with all my requests.. Thank you!

CHALLENGE – DAY 12
EMOTIONAL BALANCE

Take a moment and think of a few ways to create emotional balance in your life.

What could you do to balance your mood if you find yourself starting to have a bad day?

_____

_____

_____

_____

_____

_____

_____

What EI Secrets are important to maintaining a healthy balance, and why?

_____

_____

_____

_____

_____

_____

_____

_____

_____

_____

_____

_____

Additional Thoughts on Emotional Balance

_____
_____
_____
_____
_____
_____
_____
_____
_____
_____
_____
_____
_____
_____
_____
_____
_____
_____
_____
_____
_____
_____
_____
_____
_____
_____
_____
_____

EI Secret #13: *Emotional Preparedness*

By now you should feel some consistency in applying these EI secrets and hopefully, you should start feeling good about being emotionally intelligent. Today's secret is very powerful and will ultimately give you the superpower that will provide you with the ability to make the right decisions at the right moment when something is happening to you unexpectedly. Today's secret is about **emotional preparedness;** how to be emotionally prepared when people or situations change.

When I used to work at the probation department, we had this training they called Defensive Tactics. When you're talking to somebody in close proximity, they train you to put some space between you and that individual, just a few feet, just in case this person acts up, or decides they want to attack or rush you. It's called a defensible space. I liken that to the Emotional Intelligence process, which is why this secret is about preparing yourself to stay centered when people or things switch up on you. The way you do that is the same way they wanted us to create defensible space, meaning don't ever put yourself too close to the next person's emotions. Go into every situation with a little space in your mind. Use your situational awareness and make sure that you create a gap between those emotions and the energy that's being directed towards you. This way, if that person comes at you negatively or unexpectedly, you have the ability to side step the situation effectively.

Your mental side step is just a pause. We've learned in the bigger scope of the Emotional Intelligence program to make sure you put some space between your responses.

The secret is to stay mentally prepared and create a defensible space between the emotional flow and your actions every single day. This will help you stay emotionally prepared for when people or things switch up on you.

CHALLENGE – DAY 13
EMOTIONAL PREPAREDNESS

For the next twenty-four hours, start practicing what your mental defensible space may feel like. It could be just a brief pause in your thoughts or even a conscious thought to take a deep breath before you act or speak that gives you the space to not overreact, and the ability to respond with Emotional Intelligence.

How would taking a pause before you acted or spoke help you in a situation?

_____
_____
_____
_____
_____
_____
_____
_____
_____
_____
_____

How differently might that situation or conversation have turned out had you not taken that pause?

_____
_____
_____
_____
_____
_____
_____
_____

Additional Thoughts on Emotional Preparedness

EI Secret #14: *Emotional Mathematics*

Congrats, you are just about halfway through the challenge! Even if you've missed a couple of days, don't sweat it. Just go back and catch up at any time. The point is that you're here on Day 14, so all we have do is keep pushing.

Today's secret is one that's very similar to a previous secret we talked about when we discussed *Control, ALT, Delete* as a method to reset in the moment: Controlling your emotions, looking for alternative solutions, and deleting the toxic situation in front of you. This secret is most useful when you're looking at the whole picture. I like to call this one **emotional mathematics**.

Emotional mathematics should be used when there's a problem that needs to be solved, or when you're looking at a problem in your life. When things are not adding up, it's time to start subtracting. When things don't seem like they are in alignment like they should be, or something just doesn't make sense, instead of adding to it, you need to do some subtracting.

If a situation is not looking the way it's supposed to look, if it's not panning out the way it's supposed to pan out, if it's not in alignment with the direction that you're going, fall back.

Subtract, remove yourself from the situation, the scenario, or the conversation, because it's not adding up. *If it's not adding up, start to subtract.* It's a very simple formula that can be applied to just about every situation.

When I'm in the middle of something, such as a business project, or if I'm working with someone who is not doing what they said they would, or the business is not delivering the goods as promised, I've learned not to keep digging, not to keep giving chance after chance after chance. The responsibility is on the person or the entity that you're dealing with to own up to their end of the bargain. When they're not owning up, the best thing that you can do is fall back.

Why would you fall back? Because Emotional Intelligence is about always operating from a centered space. It's the ability to be at peace as much as you can. You can't have peace of mind if you're always giving people a piece of your mind. If it's not adding up, it's time to subtract. When you look at a problem and if things are not going the way they're supposed to go, you already know the best thing to do is back off and let it be what it's going to be. Now, here's the key when it comes to Emotional Intelligence: if it starts adding back up again, take a fresh look at it because we don't like to cut people off for good; people or situations can change. This is when emotional maturity comes into play. We need to discern when it's appropriate to subtract, have a conversation, or just unplug to reconnect.

Sometimes you have to unplug to reconnect so that you can try to get back on track. Have you ever tried to plug something into the wall and it didn't work, and you took it out and plugged it back in, then suddenly it's working again? Sometimes the energy doesn't always line up the first time, so you have to reconnect back into it at a later date. I'm not saying make drastic decisions or throw everything you've worked for away. I am saying on this quest to become emotionally intelligent, take it into consideration and think about it all and do what makes sense for that particular situation.

 bbbvaughn commented: I am EXCITED...I completed the Challenge!!!! It took me 40 days. 🫠

I had no idea how much I emotionally suffer, bury it and keep moving. This challenge has provided necessary freedom to explore my emotions, (my vulnerability) without judging, condemning or criticizing myself. I will keep the EI secrets in daily rotation...

The EI Challenge is valued opportunity - wealth on another level.

DB, I appreciate you so Damn much. Your "yes" has changed lives for the better, bless you!! 💯 💯 💯

CHALLENGE – DAY 14
EMOTIONAL MATHEMATICS

Think about some things in your life that you know that haven't been adding up, so you know if it's time to subtract. Pay attention in the next twenty-four hours to things around you that might not be adding up.

What things in your life aren't adding up?

_____
_____
_____
_____
_____
_____
_____
_____
_____

What things could you subtract, and what things do you need to unplug from to reconnect for a fresh perspective?

_____
_____
_____
_____
_____
_____
_____
_____
_____

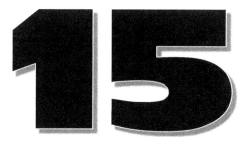

EI Secret #15: *Emotional Storyboard*

Welcome to the second half of the 30 Day Challenge!

If you remember, the Emotional Intelligence domains are driven by self-awareness, managing your reactions, situational awareness, and relationship management. This is what Emotional Intelligence is at its core, and everything else is built from there.

This particular secret is going to really fall under the self-awareness model and has to do with the "**emotional storyboard**" that's created in our heads from any particular situation that may arise. Think about when you text or call someone and they don't get back to you right away, especially if it's a family member or your significant other. We might create a story in our head about why they don't respond immediately.

Sometimes when I text my kids, especially my youngest, and they don't get back to me right away, I start telling myself a story. *He's playing games, he's seen the text but is ignoring me, and if he's going to do that then I'm going to take the phone away from him.* Like I said yesterday, if it's not adding up, I want to subtract.

But the Emotional Intelligence theory, strategy, and fundamentals say, "Be careful of the story you tell in your head." What if he didn't see the text? What if he was asleep? What if he was actually in school doing his work? What if his battery was dead? There are a lot of other variables to the story I create in my head.

There are a lot of reasons you create a story for yourself, but you want to be mindful of that. This doesn't just fall into self-awareness, this also falls under relationship management. Many people create stories in their head on this emotional storyboard about how they think the other person *should* be reacting *("He should respond to my text right away," "She should pick up my calls every time,"* etc.), and many times, they move into stealth mode emotions. They never had the necessary conversations with the other person to get clarity; instead they just ran with that story they created in their own head.

One day I was hanging out in a park and I met up with a couple of guys I knew. We were chatting for a bit, then one of the guys said, "You know I was mad at you for a minute there, DB." Surprised, I said, "Really?" I had no idea, and really thought it was a joke. But his facial expression didn't change, and my Spidey senses kicked in so I asked, "So what's up?" He went on to explain that he had read through my previous book, *iNeverWorry*, and didn't see his name mentioned. I asked him what he meant. He went into the story about how we used to hang out back in the day. "I was rockin' with you before you had all of this," which was a true statement. We grew up together, but when I wrote that book, I was not thinking about those things. The story he started telling himself was that I was acting funny and that I had forgotten where I came from, which started to probably lead into a little bit of hate and jealousy. How was I ever supposed to know all of this? Luckily, I saw him so I could clear it up, but I wonder how long that story had been going on in his head? This happens all the time. People think you should be doing something for them based on *their* needs, *their* views, *their* values, and when

78

those things don't match up, they create an emotional storyboard. A lot of times it will strain the relationship. And here is the key: the stories are going to happen regardless. Research says that we have about 50,000 thoughts going through our head every single day. They're going to come with narratives. I'm not telling you that it's wrong to have a story; I'm simply telling you to be aware of that story and any information you may not be aware of, and to be mindful of what action you may take as a result.

CHALLENGE – DAY 15
EMOTIONAL STORYBOARD

For the next twenty-four hours, revisit a time or two when you may have created stories in your head about a particular situation. Maybe you know someone else who has created one about you.

Think about a time you created a story about a particular situation. How did this hinder a particular relationship?

_____
_____
_____
_____
_____
_____
_____

How does being mindful of the stories we create about situations help us be more emotionally intelligent?

_____
_____
_____
_____
_____
_____
_____
_____
_____

Additional Thoughts on Emotional Storyboard

EI Secret #16: *Emotional Parenting*

If you have kids, you will totally understand where I'm coming from with this. This particular secret is one that you really have to be mindful of because your kids are probably the humans that can probably set you off the most, right?

Nothing gets me more upset than when my children are not doing what they're supposed to be doing; or when they do something different than what I asked them to do; or they're not being straightforward and truthful.

So, this particular secret is about **emotional parenting** because we can get really emotional while we're parenting. They didn't give us a manual about how to raise kids; you just have them, you experience them, and you do the best you can. It's very important to make sure that they are growing and experiencing life on their own terms in the best way they know how. As parents, we're in this coaching and guiding space where we're just trying to illuminate a path for them to walk where ideally the terrain is not as rough as it was for us. However, sometimes they want to take the long or hard way and they want to do it *their* way, and we have to be okay with that.

I know it's very hard for you to watch them make those mistakes but the reality is, they're going to do doing it anyway. There's no need for you to get over emotional and stress yourself out about it. Now, I also know it's definitely easier said than done. Case in point, this morning I woke up to get my son up for school, our normal routine, but this morning his door was locked. Now, he's 13, about to turn 14 later this year and he is in a different space. He's growing, he is taller than everybody in the family now and I know he's coming into himself.

So now I can't get in and he's in there dead asleep and I have to bang on the door to wake him. I've already told him several times not to lock that door. Then when I knock on the door he doesn't answer. I'm really starting to get worked up. I'm not going to lie, my first thought was, "I want to kick this door open because I told you not to lock the door." That's a natural emotion, right? But I put space between my response and my action. I also had to be mindful of the story I was telling myself. I just kept knocking until he got up. Once he got up and opened the door, I reacted a bit.

I asked him, "Why is your door locked?" He was just standing there, in a sleepy haze. I didn't even take that into consideration at first, I just started fussing at him. He said, "I don't know how the door got locked." This just made me have an even more emotional reaction, but then I had to pause and say, "You know what? Go ahead and get dressed. The door is open. That's fine. We'll talk about it later." I had to disconnect myself. I had to, even though I was bothered by him saying he didn't lock the door, my thoughts were, "Well, who the hell locked the door then?" And he was standing by that, like someone else must have come in and mysteriously locked it.

Of course, emotionally, that is going to send me up to a higher level, but remember, the higher the emotion the lower the logic. I realized that I was not going to be able to have a logical conversation with him in that moment. I was going to be in the mindset of smashing on him because who else could have locked

84

the door? It just made me think about all the other times I've had to have these conversations with him, and each one of my kids, for different things and how they just stand there and take a stance on something that is not factual. They won't just open up and come clean. The expectations we have of our children can make parenting very tough, even though one of the things I've learned is *no expectations, no disappointments*.

Stress is usually activated when our expectations don't match reality, and stress usually slides into anxiety or anger and that emotion becomes the lead in the conversation. I went to open the door, that door was locked, my stress went up, I got frustrated, frustration turned into anger, and it guided the conversation. We can go on and on about emotional parenting, but I just wanted to encourage you to be mindful when you are parenting. You're going to be emotional and when you're emotional, you are having a conversation from an emotionally charged space. Be mindful of the story you tell yourself so you don't say things to your kids that you might want to take back later, or things that are out of alignment with the ultimate goal. The goal is to get them to be better.

Always take a step back and disconnect. As soon you find yourself getting frustrated, you have to be the responsible one. Remember, you are responsible for how you act, no matter how you feel. You have to be the one to take a step back, reconnect, and do it as many times as possible so that you're in a positive mindset to get your point across. You are setting an emotionally intelligent example for them to follow.

CHALLENGE – DAY 16
EMOTIONAL PARENTING

Think about some of the things your children have done that have set you off.

How could you use Emotional Intelligence to temper your responses when your children might set you off?

_____

_____

_____

_____

_____

_____

_____

_____

_____

_____

In what ways could setting the example of using Emotional Intelligence benefit your children now and in the future?

_____

_____

_____

_____

_____

_____

_____

_____

Additional Thoughts on Emotional Parenting

_____
_____
_____
_____
_____
_____
_____
_____
_____
_____
_____
_____
_____
_____
_____
_____
_____
_____
_____
_____
_____
_____
_____
_____
_____
_____
_____
_____

EI Secret #17: *Emotional Vibrations*

This secret, even though it's late in the challenge, should not be mistaken for being less important as the other ones. Each one of these secrets is important in their own right and have to do with how you receive and deliver information. This particular secret has everything to do with **emotional vibrations**.

People speak about energy, vibes, good vibes, bad vibes, and things of that nature. If you don't believe in these phrases or if you've never given them any thought, take a moment to think about the power of energy. Energy and vibrations go hand in hand; they're essentially the same thing. The level of your energy has a direct correlation to how you're vibrating, right? Energy cannot be created or destroyed. Energy is just transferred between us day to day.

When you're in a bad mood, the next person that comes into communication or contact with you is more than likely going to feel that vibe and pick up on how you're feeling. Have you ever come across someone and you can tell something's wrong just by looking at them? The same is true with good vibes too. When someone is in a great mood, you just feel it. That's the energy they're carrying and exuding. Being conscious of emotional vibrations is being conscious of the energy that you're carrying and exuding on a day to day basis, moment to moment. If you can understand that, then you can consciously decide where and how you want to share that energy, or if you should be sharing that energy at all.

You've seen ads that talk about making sure that you drink responsibly, meaning you can drink alcohol but don't be reckless, don't drink and drive, etc. The same thing applies to emotional vibrations. We need to practice 'vibing' responsibly. You are responsible for how you act, no matter how you feel. When you come in contact with others, it is your responsibility to check in on your emotional vibrations, whether they're good, bad, or just 'meh,' and then think about you how should navigate throughout the day.

Vibing responsibly is being aware. When you come into a space where everyone is happy and upbeat and you're down with low vibes, try not to bring other people down by talking about whatever has you down. Try to attach to their good vibes and bring your level up or simply remove yourself from the situation to avoid spoiling those good vibes.

Alternatively, you could be in a really good mood and step into a space or a conversation where somebody is exhibiting low vibes and you have to decide relatively quickly whether you can pull them up to a positive vibration or if you should take a step back because they're not ready or willing to attach to your good vibes. This is very important in the Emotional Intelligence platform and falls under the domain of situational awareness - being able to really understand yourself and others; being able to distinguish when you should connect or disconnect at a moment's notice. This secret is a very powerful one. How do you tap in to emotional vibrations and understand what your mood and attitude is at all times? Are you honest about it? Pay attention, have some situational awareness to the vibrations that other people are operating in around you, so you can understand how much to embrace and how much to stay away. Protect your peace at all times.

 Raquel Wiley is 😄 feeling motivated.
Yesterday at 10:22 AM · 👥

Top of mind today, I'm focused on "Vibing Responsibly" across the board... with and on purpose and more importantly with no regrets!

One of my new nuggets from **Db Bedford** and his Emotional Intelligence platform. If you aren't familiar with his 30 Day EI Challenge I would highly encourage and recommend you to check it out!

Just when I thought I was pretty much on point ... here comes this opportunity to increase my self awareness and improve the management of my emotions both personally and professionally that is aiding me in being my best me ever!! 🙌✨

CHALLENGE – DAY 17
EMOTIONAL VIBRATIONS

Think about the emotional vibrations in your life. Think about how you've been feeling today, and in the past few days. Think about the other people around you. For the next twenty-four hours, I want you to check your emotional vibrations. Are you vibrating high? Are you vibrating low? Are you vibrating somewhere in the middle? Either one of them is okay. What you do with them is where the intelligent part comes in.

How did people around you react when you were vibrating high? Low? What about when you were somewhere in the middle?

_____
_____
_____
_____
_____
_____
_____
_____

What are some things you could do to bring up your mood when you feel low?

_____
_____
_____
_____
_____
_____
_____

Additional Thoughts on Emotional Vibrations

_____
_____
_____
_____
_____
_____
_____
_____
_____
_____
_____
_____
_____
_____
_____
_____
_____
_____
_____
_____
_____
_____
_____
_____
_____
_____
_____
_____
_____
_____
_____
_____

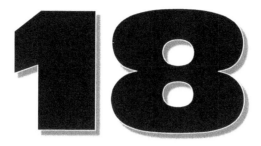

EI Secret #18: *Emotional Biases*

Today's secret is a little sensitive, and piggybacks on the vibration conversation we had in the previous chapter. It's something that we have to start being very honest about in order to move forward and grow.

I said earlier in the challenge, "What cannot be measured cannot be managed." If you can't identify your emotions, you can't measure them, which means you can't manage them. This secret is one that you may not even be aware that you have, and it is about **emotional biases**.

Recently, I was at my son's baseball game in an area that was predominately white. As I'm walking back to my truck, there was another truck parked next to me and it was surrounded by a few people. They were in a conversation, so I assumed that they probably weren't going to speak to me. I was okay with that. I was just going to pass by, but I came into the situation with a preconceived notion of how I felt about that.

So, I walked by. They didn't speak. I didn't speak. As I passed them, I sneezed, and in unison they all said, "God bless you." I responded immediately, "Why, thank you." And just like that, the energy shifted.

We carry these emotional biases with us whether we realize it or not. I think emotional bias really operates in stealth mode. Now, I'm not a racist person. I feel very confident when I say that. I love all people. I love engaging with people in general, but I also understand that when I'm in different places, in different groups, that I need to pay attention to that particular energy. Situational awareness, right? However, I also understand that I can misread the energy, that I can be biased about what that energy might be before I even feel it. In hindsight, I should've spoken, maybe said "hi," because these people were very courteous. They could've just let the moment pass when I walked past them as I sneezed, but they didn't.

Emotional biases are very important to understand; such as how you feel about other races, political parties, and social or financial statuses. You want to be careful of how you react to things that you are already against in your mind, no matter what other logic is put into play. A lot of times we're making decisions based on emotional biases. I want you to be really honest here. What are your emotional biases? Trust me, if you're biased about something, there's an emotion behind it.

For example, take our current president. Although he's just a figurehead, he is a representation of a certain type of people in this country. If you see a person wearing a "Make America Great Again" hat and you don't support Trump, is there a bias there? Is there an emotion behind that bias before you even get to know that person?

On the flip side, I wear hoodies a lot, and I usually wear all black. When white folks first see me, what are their assumptions about me? What is their experience with black men wearing hoodies? Was it something they saw on TV? Was it something they experienced on their own? What is their emotional bias and how are they judging me?

There are many ways we can go back and forth with this, but the key is to figure out the ideas within you that are emotionally biased. You may not change them because you have the right to feel the way you want to feel, but you may consider the impact it has on how you deliver information and how you receive information. You could potentially miss valuable opportunities because of your emotional biases.

I could have stopped and had a conversation with that group of people I passed at my son's baseball game. Who knows what could have come out of that conversation? While I was at the game, I also met another woman who hadn't seen me before. She wanted to know who I was, so we started talking. I found out that she's a professor at Duke University and has done some work at Howard. We started talking about racism and how it's affecting this country. We had a really good conversation and we'll probably do some work together. If I had not been open to receiving her vibe and having a conversation with her, and vice versa, we would never have discovered the beauty of when two humans connect and the resources we can bring together.

CHALLENGE – DAY 18
EMOTIONAL BIASES

Spend the next twenty-four hours reevaluating yourself and your emotional biases. Be completely honest with yourself. You don't have to change your mind about these mindsets, only how you deal with them.

What are some things you are biased about?

_____
_____
_____
_____
_____
_____
_____
_____

How might those biases hinder your personal growth and Emotional Intelligence?

_____
_____
_____
_____
_____
_____
_____
_____

How can you use Emotional Intelligence to avoid using those biases when interacting with others?

_____

_____

_____

_____

_____

_____

_____

_____

_____

_____

_____

_____

_____

_____

EI Secret #19: *Emotional Patience*

Wow, Day 19 already!

Recently I had a very interesting conversation with my homeboy. We were talking about a situation he was having at work and he was getting a little fed up with how a supervisor was conducting herself. He was really close to filing a complaint and because of how he emotionally felt about it, I advised him that it might be a good strategy to neutralize her aggressiveness.

In the end, he decided to take the high road and let the moment pass. He kept his attitude in check and just continued to deliver good work. He wound up getting moved to another manager so he didn't have to deal with that situation any longer. He felt good because he didn't have to leave a negative footprint behind. It just worked itself out. There's no negativity associated with the situation, and he can just continue to do his work and move on. Often times, especially at work where colleagues or supervisors can get under our skin, people are quick to get aggressive in response to some interaction then create this big old drama-filled environment when the moment will just pass without intervention.

I was sharing a story with him about some business I was doing with an organization and the key person isn't really good at getting back to me. If I email her, she won't email back at all. Later, out of the blue, she'll email me and say she has two business leads for me, and they always turn out to be quality leads.

There were a few times I felt that story start in my head; "I emailed you a couple of times. Why didn't you respond?!" But that's just not how she moves. Again, we talked about the stories you create in your head. I have to remind myself to recognize that this is just how she operates and to be patient.

Today's secret is about **emotional patience**. In the heat of the moment when you don't feel like being patient and you feel like saying something, taking action, or throwing away a relationship, be patient. Sometimes it comes back around. Sometimes you don't need to leave a footprint.

Now, I don't want to confuse this with some of the conversations we've had about vibrating on a higher frequency and disconnecting from toxic situations. When something is toxic, you definitely want to do your best to elevate above it and disconnect. In each one of these situations there was a level of disconnect, but it was *how* we disconnected that mattered. We didn't disconnect and throw up the bird or say something slick or create bad energy. It was simply, "Okay, even though I feel a certain kind of way, I'm not going to take any action." This was the appropriate thing to do in that particular situation.

How many times in life have you taken action in an emotional moment, but if you had been patient the situation would've worked itself out? Take emotional patience into consideration. In that moment where you don't want to be patient, check your emotions. You can still feel the way you want to feel about it, but just be patient and confident that the situation will correct itself one way or another.

102

The reality is that everybody has a right to be as right or as wrong as they choose to be. We've got to get out of the habit of trying to make people be the way we want them to be. Accept life for what it is, not how you would like it to be.

CHALLENGE – DAY 19
EMOTIONAL PATIENCE

Pay attention to your patience level today and the emotions behind it.

Think of a time you may have taken rash action in an emotional moment, but if you had been patient, the situation would've worked itself out. How differently would things have been?

_____
_____
_____
_____
_____
_____
_____
_____

What other EI secrets could you use to exercise emotional patience to its fullest potential?

_____
_____
_____
_____
_____
_____
_____
_____
_____
_____

Additional Thoughts on Emotional Patience

EI Secret #20: *Taking Things Personally*

This secret is one that trips us up a lot. It's definitely associated with those stealth mode emotions and is probably one of the most controversial. People go back and forth with me about this one quite often. I understand why; when I mention this secret, they do exactly what this secret tells them not to do. Today's secret is about **taking things personally**.

I'm quite sure when I say, "Stop take things personally," the first thing that comes to mind is, "Well, what about this? And what if they do that? And how could I not take this personally when they were personally talking to me?"

What I've learned is that I need to remember, at all times, that I'm looking at the world through the lens of Emotional Intelligence. If I'm going to operate in that space, then I quickly understand that I shouldn't take things personally even when it *feels* personal. The reason you're able to do that is because people are existing with or without you. Right now, the person that you are probably frustrated with, who's done something to you that you've taken personally, has probably done it to countless others – you're not the only one. I'm willing to bet that if I had a drone that followed that person around for a day or two, you would see that same behavior show up in other places. You would quickly realize that you're not that special. Unfortunately, we don't have the luxury of following someone around when we are in line at the DMV when the agent is rude to us, or when we experience bad customer service at the grocery store, or when we're not seeing eye to eye with a coworker.

You're not looking at it logically if you're taking it personally. Emotional Intelligence is about intelligence and not emotions. If you look at the situation logically, you start to think about who you are as a person, and if you've done something in that situation to elicit some type of reaction. Then Emotional Intelligence and the self- awareness piece of it brings you back to a space where you own it. If you absolutely didn't do anything to warrant the response that person is exhibiting, then you know it really has nothing to do with you. It's not personal. It's a reflection of *them* and *their* behavior. Most people's actions are a direct reflection of them. When a situation happens to you such as your car didn't start this morning, somebody breaks into your car, or you get sick, it's not personal, right?

If you watched the news this morning, I'll bet there were a lot of random tragedies that happened. There are fires, car accidents, gunshots, and more. All this stuff happens every day, so I feel lucky that none of those things happened to me today. But if it ever does happen to me, it's not personal because the world is existing and moving with or without me.

I understand this is a very difficult one for people to take in. The ability to not take things personally is a challenge in and of itself. But if you can accomplish that, all the rest of these secrets will fall right in line and you'll be so much freer. That's why it's important to get up every day, look at the world through the lens of EI and embrace the world for what it has to offer *for today*. Accept things for what they are, not how we would like them to be. Embrace the day because whether it's a good day or a bad day, it is the only day that we have.

 Travis Loveless ▶ **iNeverWorry Academy**
45 mins · 🖼

Still at it! I have been quiet on FB because life has become a little hectic. I make time for this challenge though :).

I have been spending time learning to not take it personal, and wow does life feel a lot less heavy emotionally. I was able to show my girlfriend this one, and it truly is a great secret. In fact I was able to also use behavior detection to help her identify a situation in traffic later on that she got upset about, and SHE was able to use EI to not take it personal!!!

Thank you again, DB!

Peace

CHALLENGE – DAY 20
TAKING THINGS PERSONALLY

Today, practice not taking things personally. Think about whether you are someone who takes things personally. Can you make that adjustment? Trust me, if you can embrace this one, you will free yourself and you will move a lot lighter in any situation.

Think about something that happened today that you might have taken personally. How might you have turned that around and not taken it personally?

_____
_____
_____
_____
_____
_____
_____
_____
_____

How does not taking things personally further your personal Emotional Intelligence?

_____
_____
_____
_____
_____
_____
_____
_____
_____

Additional Thoughts on Taking Things Personally

EI Secret #21: *The Emotional Beast*

Today's secret had me thinking about a secret that's actually been a lifesaver for me. I was in juvenile hall and there was this counselor we used to call The Old Wise Man. He had some game for me because I had a real anger problem back in the day. It didn't take much for me to get really upset over the littlest things and then explode. At times, I was ready to go all in, ready to give up every single thing I had worked for.

I didn't start to get a better handle on my behavior and my anger until he told me this story. The Old Wise Man said to me, "You know what, DB? I was just like you. Man, I have a very serious temper, and it's like a beast...and it's inside of all of us." Today's secret is entitled **emotional beast**. I want you to pay attention to the emotional beast that probably lies inside of you, too.

The Old Wise Man continued to tell me his story. "DB, you know, this beast, if I let him stand up, at eight feet tall and 300 pounds with his rock-solid muscle, it's going to be hard for me to calm him down. I have to wait until he gets tired or he decides to calm down. This beast is inside of me, asleep, every single day. Sometimes there are things that happen in a day that lightweight disturb him and make him want to wake up, so he might start

113

turning over in his sleep, you know what I mean? He has to calm himself down and I have to pat him back to sleep like, 'no, go on and lay back down. We don't want you to get up.' Sometimes, he even makes it up to his knees, like he's about to stand up, and then he'll calm himself down and I'll be thankful that he didn't get up."

He gave me this visual to think about when it comes to controlling our anger and managing that emotional beast inside of each one of us. I know when I get angry, and one of the reasons why I'm so adamant about this Emotional Intelligence platform, I'm no good once I get upset. You know, I do Emotional Intelligence for myself and it works so well for me that I had to share it with you. My history has proven that it works. My anger is not something I'm proud of, but it's something I recognize.

I was in the sixth grade and I lost my temper over a kickball game. Next thing I know, I was fighting over something silly and I was banging this kid's head on the concrete. I lost all control. The cold part about a rage is there might be a moment where you think you feel good, but there's never been a time that I have lost my temper and then afterwards thought, "Yep, I'm proud of that." Never.

You can even give your own beast a name. I just refer to it as the emotional beast. But give it a name, give it a character. Visualize what will happen if that beast in you stands all the way up. It's like the Incredible Hulk, when David Banner used to turn into the big green beast. Once he transformed into the Hulk, nobody could stop him. I'll bet that beast inside of you, when he or she wakes up, is hard to stop, too. The best thing to do is to not let that beast stand all the way up. Once he or she does, they start to get really destructive, and there's not much you can do about it once they're unleashed. You're going to have to wait until you get tired, or that beast decides to calm down. Then we have to look back at all the damage that was done along the way and do damage control. Life is too short for all that!

114

One of the keys to being emotionally intelligent is understanding that we all have an emotional beast and recognizing how to control it. Hopefully, yours has been hibernating for some time. I can proudly say that mine has been hibernating for a really long time now, and I don't ever want him to wake up. I keep him calm and comfortable so he doesn't wake up and go into a rage.

So, that's your secret for today. Monitor that emotional beast inside of you and come on back tomorrow. You're almost there. There are only a few days left! I appreciate you, I really do. If you're still here, you're well on your way to completing this challenge even if you had to go back and catch up on a few days. It's all good.

CHALLENGE - DAY 21
THE EMOTIONAL BEAST

For the next twenty-four hours, think about the emotional beast that may reside within you. Think about some occasions when you might have let that beast wake up.

What happened when you let that beast stand all the way up? What was the end result of unleashing that beast?

_____
_____
_____
_____
_____
_____
_____
_____
_____
_____
_____
_____
_____
_____

What happened when you saw the emotional beast come out in someone else? What kind of path of destruction did it create?

_____
_____
_____
_____
_____
_____

How different might the outcomes of those situations have been, had you or the other person kept that emotional beast asleep? In what ways might you keep that beast quiet?

_____

_____

_____

_____

_____

_____

_____

EI Secret #22: *Behavior Detection*

I'm so glad that you're continuing along on this Emotional Intelligence journey. Today's secret is another great one, but first let's do a quick recap.

Emotional Intelligence awareness continues to rise, and you're going to hear more and more people talk about it, especially in the workforce. I read that in the 1990's, two college students spoke on the subject and in 1995 Daniel Goleman coined the phrase 'Emotional Intelligence' in his book. After that, several people touched on the subject, including myself.

How many people, however, just throw the term "emotionally intelligent" out there? It may be the "in" thing, but they don't truly know what it means. Common sense may tell them that it must be about being smart about how they feel. Emotional Intelligence includes those four domains that we've talked about. If you were asked what Emotional Intelligence is by a potential employer, you would be able to answer this quite easily: *"Emotional Intelligence is self-awareness, managing your reactions, situational awareness, and relationship management.*

It's our personal competencies. It has everything to do with how we feel, and what we do with those feelings."

Today's secret is called **behavior detection**. Situational awareness and relationship management will fall in line within the domains of social competencies. When you get up every day and look at the world through this lens of Emotional Intelligence, you are intentionally connecting with people in a positive space. Self-awareness is like you are in the business of making people feel good about connecting to you, because you're going to lead with good energy, you're going to lead in a higher frequency, and you're going to be the person that sheds a light on their emotions wherever you go.

Behavior detection is really zoning in on the behaviors of people around you. Start paying attention, not in the end when somebody makes you upset, but in general. When you come in contact with somebody wherever you are, stranger or otherwise, observe their behavior. This will give you clues to how you want to engage with that person, if you need to. It will give you clues to what might be going on in the environment you are in, and it will help you raise your awareness using Emotional Intelligence.

I like to listen to people when they are in line at places like the grocery store or the DMV if they're complaining about stuff. I listen to what is rubbing them the wrong way. Wherever I happen to be, I just watch people's behavior, because the way to become really high level on the Emotional Intelligence scale is to look at the world, the landscape in which you navigate, every day. It really is one big classroom. Everyone is so into their feelings they don't even realize it. If you're able to realize those feelings and then know when to connect, what to connect to and what to disconnect from, you're a sharper person in this Emotional Intelligence realm.

Embrace behavior detection moving forward, and because you're pretty deep into this challenge by now, you should be well on

120

your way to being pretty adept at managing your own emotions. Start paying attention to other people's behaviors and emotions, but don't judge and don't draw conclusions (storyboarding). Just identify what might be happening. Trust me, when you start looking at the world this way, you're already on top of the game.

CHALLENGE - DAY 22
BEHAVIOR DETECTION

Next time you're talking to your supervisor, colleague, significant other or your kids, observe their behavior. Listen to their emotions. It's going to help you to effectively navigate using Emotional Intelligence, and you'll know what to do from there.

What EI secrets might you use to complement behavior detection when a conversation with a coworker starts out negatively?

_____
_____
_____
_____
_____
_____
_____
_____
_____
_____
_____
_____
_____
_____
_____
_____
_____
_____
_____
_____

Additional Thoughts on Behavior Detection

EI Secret #23: *Emotional Distractions*

We are getting pretty close to the end, so I want to talk about something else that might be holding you back from becoming emotionally intelligent. It might even be holding you back in life in general. Today's EI secret is about **emotional distractions**. What are the things that you are emotionally connected to that are distractions?

Say you are looking to lose weight or be healthier. If you are attached to eating certain junk foods or maybe drinking alcohol, there's an emotion attached to that. When you crave something, whether it's sugar, alcohol, carbs, whatever, there is an emotional feeling that comes with that craving. When you fulfill that craving, think about how you feel. *"Mmm, this is so good."* But what just happened? That craving just distracted you from your goal of losing weight or getting healthier because adding that candy, drink, fries, or whatever to your eating plan does not move you towards your goal.

Say you are looking to save money to buy a house or car but shopping really makes you feel good. If you let yourself be emotionally distracted from your goal of saving money for that house or car, you're giving in to that temporary "feel good" emotion. It is very challenging to eliminate distractions that you enjoy.

It's important to recognize these distractions as they come up, take a pause, and get back on track. It takes practice and mindfulness, but it's worth it and you can do it. Keep your focus and stay away from those hooks!

 Wilmakeepnitreal Miller ▶ **Emotional Intelligence for Women**
Just now ·

Good Morning Everyone
I just wanted to let y'all know that the Emotional Distractions is such a fact in your day to day life. Almost every time you set your goals and time frame that you want to get there it's always one thing or another to have you side step right off your course.. When setting goals i need to stay focused and on course.. To making it happen 👍 stop thinking about it and be about it 👏 That's just me i don't know about anybody else. Have a Blessed and a Fabulous weekend Everyone..
I wanna Thank you Db this Morning for waking my game back up.. Stop being distracted by things that i can do any time.. Blessings

CHALLENGE – DAY 23
EMOTIONAL DISTRACTIONS

Today's challenge is to think about what might be emotionally distracting you. Figure out what it is that makes distraction worth it to you as opposed to focusing on the goal that you're trying to achieve. More than likely, these things have emotional connections for you. Find a way to focus on the things that are the bigger goal and things that will bring you more satisfaction.

How can you refocus yourself when you find yourself distracted?

_____
_____
_____
_____
_____
_____
_____

Listen to other people in your life. What are some of the things that they are emotionally distracted by?

_____
_____
_____
_____
_____
_____
_____
_____

El Secret #24: *Week One Recap*

Welcome to Day 24, we are in the home stretch!

I want to take a moment to pause and reflect because it's important not to just skim through this stuff. I want to be very intentional about the opportunity to really learn these secrets and embrace what it's going to feel like being emotionally intelligent. The challenge today is not necessarily a secret, but a recap of week one so you have an opportunity to reflect.

On Day One we covered **emotional willingness** and we asked ourselves, "Am I emotionally willing to exercise Emotional Intelligence when I need it the most?" This is most important when those challenging times come up; when your mood is off. Are you willing? Do you have the emotional willingness to push through when it gets tough? Day One was about checking your emotional willingness and getting you ready for not only this challenge, but moving forward, looking at the world through the lens of Emotional Intelligence.

Day Two we talked about **stealth mode emotions**; emotions that we all might have when we are bothered by something but we choose not to speak on it. If we choose not to, that's okay; but in doing so, we run the risk of letting our attitude and behavior reflect how we're feeling. Others may feel something is off and we may send mixed signals, causing a breakdown in communication.

On Day Three, we talked about being able to reset ourselves with **Control, ALT, Delete**. We need to make sure we *control* our emotions, look for *alternatives*, and *delete* any toxic situations. That's a powerful secret because it gives us the ability to reset at a moment's notice when we need it most.

We then talked about not **biting the hook**. I used the analogy of a fish in the water, minding his own business, then the hook drops in front of him and he bites it. He gets snatched out of his environment, never to return. There are emotional situations, or hooks, in front of us every day that distract us from our goals that we can avoid. Remind yourself to watch for those hooks in life.

Day Five was about **emotional maturity**, growing into a space of being emotionally intelligent. Emotional maturity is different than the maturity that people think comes with age. You can be 55 years old and have little or no emotional maturity, so check your emotional maturity levels right now. If you have been dedicated to this challenge and you've been really taking these secrets to heart, more than likely your emotional maturity has grown since Day One.

On Day Six we talked about that **emotional baggage**. It's the stuff that we pick up over the course of our lives, the energy that we pick up every single day, the emotional stuff we don't unpack and carry with us. Just like when you carry luggage through the airport, you can get to your destination faster if you have nothing to weigh you down. It's the same with emotions. Sometimes we stack these emotions on top of each other and it becomes heavy on our minds and conscience. Be mindful of emotional baggage.

We rounded off Week One with **emotional grudges,** which comes with the emotional baggage. If you're carrying emotional baggage, you might also be holding on to some grudges. It's like taking poison and expecting the other person to die. Often, when you're upset with somebody or something, that person is not even thinking about you. We want to be careful with those emotional grudges because they lower our vibration. They make us lower our ability to see and think clearly, then we can't be available for everything that life has to offer.

iNEVERW⊕RRY
EMOTIONAL INTELLIGENCE

Danita Lee
Yesterday at 1:53 PM ·

Stealth Mode Emotions. Wow this is an eye opener for me. I am usually vocal about my feelings and emotions but lately I have been operating in stealth mode with two of my family members. I try to be pleasant with family even when someone has crossed the line and said something hurtful. Stealth mode has me questioning our relationship. I realize by avoiding the uneasy conversation, I may be making the situation worse. I keep thinking about what cannot be measured, cannot be managed.

CHALLENGE - DAY 24
WEEK ONE RECAP

What does being *emotionally willing* mean to you?

_____

_____

_____

_____

What do *stealth mode emotions* mean to you?

_____

_____

_____

_____

What does *Control, ALT, Delete* mean to you?

_____

_____

_____

_____

What does *biting the hook* mean to you?

_____

_____

_____

_____

What does *emotional maturity* mean to you?

_____
_____
_____
_____

What does *emotional baggage* mean to you?

_____
_____
_____
_____

What do *emotional grudges* mean to you?

_____
_____
_____
_____

EI Secret #25: *Week Two Recap*

At the beginning of Week Two, we talked about **emotional growth**. I talked about maturity and growing emotionally and essentially, it just means that you understand you've got feelings, you understand how you feel about things today, you might not feel the same way tomorrow. How you receive things today, might not be the same way you receive them tomorrow, so be in tune with your emotions and let them be what they're going to be. Don't fight them. Identify and manage them because what cannot be measured cannot be managed.

We then talked about **emotional attachments**, the "I have to do this, I have to do that." Every time something comes up, you might be attaching yourself to it, or every time you hear about something that will drive you crazy, you might react. You've got to be mindful of what you are emotionally attaching yourself to. If you're going to live intentionally with your emotions, then you want to be emotionally attaching yourself to positive things, such as your goals. Stay in alignment and avoid those emotional distractions along the way.

We also talked about **emotional confusion**. They say a confused mind will always say no. If something seems confusing or unclear, we'll usually move away from it and go on to the next. It's the same with our emotions. It's difficult to come to a solution when you are emotionally confused about something. We may just shut down and say, "Nope, I'm moving on to the next thing" instead of dealing with the problem at hand.

We talked about **emotional procrastination** because this is something we all suffer from to a certain degree. When you learn to recognize there's an emotion behind procrastination, you can move forward. There are things that you know you need to do around the house. You may not feel like doing them because you'd rather be doing something else. Perhaps vacuuming is not the most enjoyable thing for you. If you understand that by deciding to clean up something and you think about how the house is going to look after it's cleaned up, if you can attach a feeling to the end result, maybe you won't procrastinate as much.

We discussed **emotional balance;** being able to tip the scales. You don't always want to be too up or too down. You're going to have different variations of your emotions in your life, but the thing is just to keep a balance, to be on an even keel. Emotions will catch up to you and you want to make sure that they're not weighing too heavy on you. If you're always too excited and bright eyed and bushy tailed, you might miss some important stuff when you need to be a little more serious and attentive. If you're always down with low vibrations and depressed and angry and sad, you'll miss out on the beautiful things in life.

We then talked about **emotional preparedness;** consciously being prepared for people or things to possibly switch up on you because there's a good chance that they will. If you go into the day knowing and believing it's a possibility, you will be that much more emotionally prepared. You may not feel so wronged all the time. The reason people may feel wronged is either they have the desire to always be right or they have an expectation. No expectations, no disappointments. Just let things be what they're going to be and manage however the situation turns out.

We talked about **emotional mathematics**. If things are not adding up, start subtracting. If things are not going the way that you want it to go, pull back from them. If there are people in your life that are bringing you down who are toxic, or aren't healthy for you, pull back from them. We have control of who we allow to have access to us.

Angel Lowe
2 hrs · 🌐

I am responsible for my actions regardless of how I feel! So today I decided to complete Emotional Intelligence Certificate Course so from this day moving forward "I know better so I WILL DO BETTER!!"
Thank you Db Bedford for such an AMAZING program see you soon.

CHALLENGE - DAY 25
WEEK TWO RECAP

What does *emotional growth* mean to you?

_____
_____
_____
_____

What do *emotional attachments* mean to you?

_____
_____
_____
_____

What does *emotional confusion* mean to you?

_____
_____
_____
_____

What does *emotional procrastination* mean to you?

_____
_____
_____
_____

What does *emotional balance* mean to you?

_____
_____
_____
_____

What does *emotional preparedness* mean to you?

_____
_____
_____
_____

What do *emotional mathematics* mean to you?

_____
_____
_____
_____

EI Secret #26: *Week Three Recap*

It's Day 26 and we're on the move. We're about to close out and hopefully you're feeling as strong and vibrant and as emotionally intelligent as you can be in this moment. You have come a long way.

Before you started, you committed to be emotionally willing, to be open to this experience. Along the way, when those challenging situations came up that might have questioned your Emotional Intelligence, you pushed through. Now I want you to ask yourself how you've been doing. It's okay if you have mis-stepped along the way, because remember, we're going to make mistakes. Emotional Intelligence is not about this warm and fuzzy lifestyle, it is about being able to look at emotional situations through a logical lens. That is the core of Emotional Intelligence.

Let's recap Week Three. We started Week Three being mindful of the **emotional storyboard**, the stories that we tell ourselves about situations around us. Be mindful of the stories that you tell yourself when something happens that didn't quite go your way. Keep your mind open. I want you to think about the story and don't let that story start to vibrate out of control.

We then delved into **emotional parenting.** As parents we can get really emotional when dealing with our children; parenting is a tough job. We weren't given a fool-proof, one-size-fits-all manual when they were born. We have to be ok with our kids learning their own way, too, even if that way seems to be the most difficult way. They will test our emotional patience, and it can be easy to create storyboards when they misbehave. Be mindful of acting from emotionally charged spaces. It's important to remember to step back and disconnect to reconnect.

We also talked about **emotional vibrations**. We exude emotional vibrations based on how we feel, and it's easy to pick up on those vibes – good, bad, and meh. When we step into a room or situation, we need to gauge the vibrations present so that we can act accordingly. We also need to tap into our own moods throughout the day to ensure we are vibing responsibly for effective communication and successful relationships.

We then talked about **emotional biases**, those beliefs and values that have an impact on how you show up every day and how you handle situations. These emotional biases are those prejudices, those things that you just automatically consider to be distasteful. You may not even know why you feel that way. Perhaps you are doing things that your parents taught you to do and you're passing them on to your kids. They can be simple things like a distaste for a certain food, or something extreme and potentially damaging like racial or gender biases. We want to pay attention to those.

In week three, we also talked about **emotional patience.** When we have to wait for something or something's not happening when we want it to happen, we all get that little feeling of impatience. That emotion in there starts to drive how long we're willing to wait, and how you're going to engage. There are a lot of things that come with that emotional patience. Think about the feelings that come with that. All these different elements help us stay in an Emotional Intelligence state. Take the time to think about what's actually happening. If we can identify it, we can manage it.

We then discussed **taking things personally.** We talked about personalizing stuff and how it's so easy to take things personally, especially when things involve your family or your close friends. B-Legit, a good friend of mine, told me that your family and friends have the code to your emotions. They are the ones that are usually going to get you upset relatively fast. They are around you the most and they know what buttons to push, whether they're pushing them intentionally or not. Emotion is that one thing that we cannot avoid; therefore, Emotional Intelligence is something that we must have. With that, we really have to learn to not take things personally.

We ended the week with **emotional beast.** Everybody has that proverbial beast inside of us. When things start bothering us and rubbing us the wrong way, we want to imagine that when that beast stands up, it's seven feet tall and the strongest person we know. He is hard to calm down, and you know that it's going to be destructive when he stands up. If we keep that image in our heads, then we will likely do everything we can to keep him in hibernation mode.

CHALLENGE - DAY 26
WEEK THREE RECAP

What do *emotional storyboards* mean to you?

_____
_____
_____
_____

What does *emotional parenting* mean to you?

_____
_____
_____
_____

What do *emotional vibrations* mean to you?

_____
_____
_____
_____

What do *emotional biases* mean to you?

_____
_____
_____
_____

What does *emotional patience* mean to you?

_____

_____

_____

_____

What does *not taking it personally* mean to you?

_____

_____

_____

_____

What does *the emotional beast* mean to you?

_____

_____

_____

_____

Additional Thoughts on Week Three Recap

EI Secret #27: *Emotional Attitude*

As we get close to the end, it's important for me to remind you that Emotional Intelligence is about you, not necessarily about other people. There are skills here that allow you to manage your responses toward the behaviors of others, but Emotional Intelligence is really about you. The more you can embrace this as a mindset, the more you will realize that every time there is some type of difficult situation in your life, you always have to start with yourself.

So many people spend so much time looking out the window instead of looking in the mirror. It's very important to keep the lens on yourself, which is why the first domain in Emotional Intelligence is self-awareness. You need to always be conscious of what you're feeling, what your vibration is. This next secret is going to hone right in on your **emotional attitude**.

Everybody gets an attitude from time to time, it's normal. Either you're going to have a good attitude or a bad attitude, there is no in between. We are usually in a good mood or a bad mood. What kind of mood are you in right now? Your mood is in direct correlation to how you're going to receive information and how you're going to deliver information as well.

What would people say about your attitude? If you were a fly on the wall and there was a room full of people that were talking about your attitude, what would they say?

Now what does 'emotional' attitude mean? It is the way that you feel about yourself. Are you always in your feelings? Usually people who have poor attitudes take things personally. They may suffer from confirmation biases, where they take in information in a way that is primarily self-serving. They also may not take into consideration what's going on with other people. These are the things that lower the vibrations of themselves and those around them.

And here's a funny thing about people with attitudes: like bad attitudes, they seem to think that other people should just accept that this is how they are. We talked earlier about vibing responsibly. When your attitude is off track it disrupts the energy of whatever space you step into. You want to be mindful of how your attitude directly impacts your family, your friends, and your success. If you are not as successful as you'd like to be in any area of your life, perhaps an attitude check-up is in order.

There is a saying, "Your attitude determines your altitude." How you feel determines how far you will go. People only want to be around others with positive attitudes. Think about the people around you that have bad attitudes. You don't look forward to coming in contact with them because you spend a lot of energy to deal with them. It's too draining, and half the time it's not even worth it.

Today we're going to turn the lens on ourselves. We're going to start looking more in the mirror, and less out the window. Every day, ask yourself, "What is my attitude for the day?" As your day progresses, check in with yourself. What is your attitude at that moment? Keep the word 'attitude' prominent in your daily thought process, especially your emotional attitude. We want to put the word emotion in front of 'attitude' because most of our attitudes are fueled by emotions.

CHALLENGE - DAY 27
EMOTIONAL ATTITUDE

For the next twenty-four hours, check yourself so you don't wreck yourself, as the saying goes. Then after you take a look in the mirror at your own attitude, pay attention to the attitudes of others. The world of Emotional Intelligence is like one big learning ground, and we're paying attention to others for the purpose of learning. Not to critique, not to judge or gossip, but to learn what to embrace, what could be done better, and how we can optimize our performance every day, in every area of our life.

How was your attitude today?

_____
_____
_____
_____

If you experienced some lows in your attitude, what did you do to bring yourself back up? Would you do anything differently next time?

_____
_____
_____
_____
_____

In your observations of others, how might bad attitudes affect relationships and opportunities? Was there anything you could have done to change the situation?

_____

_____

_____

_____

_____

EI Secret #28: *What is Your Why?*

I consider each one of these elements I've shared with you secrets. You could ask somebody, "Have you ever heard of emotional grudges?" and more than likely they will not know what you're talking about. Most people will not be able to put a framework around their behaviors, which is why it becomes a secret; unidentified emotions can never be managed. You cannot manage what you cannot measure, so when you have this secret, you get a one up in the elements.

By now, you should be feeling good. You probably have talked to a couple of people about some of these secrets. We went over emotional attitudes in the previous chapter, and hopefully you took some time to be honest about your attitude. If you're in a good mood most of the time, that's good, but even the most upbeat people get into bad moods, it's only natural. Sometimes we just wake up in a funk and we have to reset. We have to disconnect to reconnect.

But in order to be truly successful in this challenge and in life, in our relationships, in our finances, with our health, we're going to have to ask ourselves, "**What is my 'why'?**" Why do you do what you do?

An old wise man once said that the two most important days of our lives is the day we were born and the day we discover why. Sadly, some of us will exit this life without ever discovering our why. You have to start peeling back the layers to discover your purpose because all of us have a purpose, a gift.

Why is this important? I discovered 25 years ago that my 'why' was to serve people. I was a coach, a mentor, an advocate, a thought leader in whatever space I was in. I discovered this when I was in the deepest and darkest space of my life; when I was on my way to prison. It was brought to my attention by Judge Larry Goodman, who could have sent me to the penitentiary easily, but decided to challenge me for self-discovery. When I started to reverse engineer my life and look back, I actually noticed all these different places where I was being a leader. People always turned to me for some perspective, so I owned that space and realized I really loved and enjoyed doing that.

Here's the key element to this. Once I not only discovered my purpose but embraced it and lived it, my whole world opened up and I no longer found myself chasing anything. Since then I have been attracting everything that this world has for me, which means that all I have to do is stay in my purpose, stay in my 'why', do what I was brought here to do, and everything that I need or want that helps move that agenda along comes to me. I don't have to go searching for it. This is why I want you to discover your 'why'. This is why I want you to be honest about your purpose. Don't be discouraged if it takes some time. Have patience but stay focused.

How do you discover it? Start looking at the things that you naturally know how to do. Start thinking about the things that you love doing, that bring you joy. Then take a look at what others say that you're good at. What do other people admire

154

about you? What do other people tell you that you are a natural at? You could naturally know how to fix stuff, but if you don't love it, it might not be your purpose. Those three things need to line up.

Here's the catch with this. You might decide to not work at your current job once you discover your purpose. Or, you might have to revisit the relationship that you're in. You may have to disconnect from some of the friends that you have because you only want to be in alignment with the people that are going in your same direction and believe in you and the direction that you're going.

Tete Denise
Sunday at 7:41 PM ·

I have truly been mastering peace lately ! and its so amazing! there is no way to make life perfect or go smoothly but we can control our perspectives and how we handle people & situations! Please look into **Db Bedford** platform of iNeverWorry ! He has an amazing book & other tools that can help you enhance skills that are necessary as humans !

Its worth the work !! 💪

155

CHALLENGE - DAY 28
WHAT IS YOUR WHY?

Today's challenge is to ask yourself, "What's my 'why'?" Take a moment. Right it down.

What do I enjoy doing?

_____

_____

_____

_____

_____

_____

_____

What do others say I'm good at doing?

_____

_____

_____

_____

_____

_____

_____

_____

Based on the above, what may my 'why' be? What can I do to pursue it?

_____

_____

_____

_____

_____

Additional Thoughts on What is Your 'Why'?

EI Secret #29: *Emotional Acceptance*

Today's secret is about **emotional acceptance**. What I have found in my work and in my travels and all the different people that I've coached, trained, and listened to, one thing is pretty consistent. They all talk about and struggle with acceptance. What happens is that your beliefs get in the way of the information that's coming towards you. When things are happening, when people are telling you things or sharing things with you, you struggle with accepting it if your beliefs conflict with the information coming in. When you struggle with accepting something, it tends to raise your stress level. If it raises your stress level, your emotions can slide into frustration, and sometimes into anger. Then as all those things - stress, frustration, anger - are happening, your vibrations are getting lower.

When your vibrations are low, your clarity and bandwidth are shutting down. One of the ways to keep your bandwidth wide, your clarity as clear as possible, and your frequency high, is to learn to accept. Now accepting things means that you're just accepting it for what it is, not what you would like it to be. That's the key. The minute you start trying to change the element forcefully, the tree branches break.

Sometimes you can influence change by simply developing a different perspective. But if you find yourself with some turbulence in a flight plan simply because you won't accept what's being said or what's happening, then your job is to understand that this is a case of emotional acceptance, meaning you feel a certain kind of way; therefore, you can't accept it for what it is.

All of these secrets and information nuggets can be life changing. You just have to identify those times where would they be the most relevant and then apply them. You can't make excuses. You can't learn all these secrets and then tell me they don't work if you don't apply them. Apply them first. Give them a fair shot. Go in with the right emotional attitude about a situation and see what happens. I guarantee that you are going to increase your situational awareness. The only promise that I'm making in this challenge is that from day one when you said you were emotionally willing to be open to Emotional Intelligence, is that you will be emotionally intelligent.

Being emotionally intelligent is an ongoing lifelong process, so there is no finish line. How do I qualify you as emotionally intelligent? Consider times when you feel like you're not managing your reactions, you're not being self-aware, maybe you lose your cool. If you have the ability to bounce back, to get back into a restorative process relatively quickly, I would then consider you to be someone who operates in an emotionally intelligent space. We won't always get it right. Quite honestly, we would set ourselves up for failure if we expected to be right 100% of the time. What we're doing here is preparing ourselves to bounce back strong when things go wrong.

CHALLENGE - DAY 29
EMOTIONAL ACCEPTANCE

Think about the things that you struggle to accept. Pay attention to the people around you.

What are you struggling to accept?

_____
_____
_____
_____
_____
_____
_____
_____
_____
_____

What things do others close to you seem to struggle to accept? How could you use Emotional Intelligence to turn that around?

_____
_____
_____
_____
_____
_____
_____
_____
_____
_____
_____
_____

EI Secret #30: *Congrats!*

Congratulations! You made it to Day 30 of the Emotional Intelligence Challenge. You just went through 30 days of taking in powerful life-changing Emotional Intelligence secrets. You've been processing them, reflecting on yourself, then taking a look at others and applying these secrets to your daily life. How do you feel? You should feel good. It doesn't matter if you did the 30 days consecutively or if it took you 45 days. The point is that you did 30 days of embracing Emotional Intelligence secrets, which makes you more emotionally Intelligent than most people around you, in every situation that you step into. That's definitely something to be proud of.

Many people don't even know about Emotional Intelligence yet, and if they do, very few can articulate what it means. Most people couldn't tell you the four domains of Emotional Intelligence, but you can: self-awareness, managing your reactions, situational awareness, and managing relationships. You understand that self-awareness and managing your reactions are the personal competencies in the process.

How do I feel? That's the emotion. What do you do with that feeling? That's the intelligence part. You've learned that the core fundamental of being emotionally intelligent is the ability to process emotionally charged situations through a logical lens. We learned that when emotions are high, logic is low. The higher the emotion, the lower the logic.

How do you move forward now; where do you go from here? How do you show up and be emotionally intelligent? You're going to get up every single day and remember that you are responsible for how you act, no matter how you feel.

Once you acknowledge whoever it is that you pray to, you should give thanks and have some gratitude. Gratitude is very important, we should all be grateful just for being alive. The easiest thing to do is to remember that you are supposed to be operating from a centered space; peace, with your emotional balance intact. And how does that happen? It happens by taking time to keep your mental battery charged throughout the day.

You're going to put some space between your responses, you're going to make sure that you don't start the day with expectations, you're going to stay emotionally prepared for people or situations that may switch up on you. You're going travel light and stay baggage free. So, when things happen to you throughout the day, you're going to emotionally process it, because when you emotionally process things, you increase your chances of making things come out in a positive way.

I'm so excited that you made it through the challenge. Emotional Intelligence is the number one asset that employers are going to be looking for in the years to come, and you're ahead of the game already. You should be in a better space; at home, with your children, with your family and friends. Remember: no matter what comes your way, from the extreme to the minimal, the key is, when you get up every day, you're looking at the world through this lens of Emotional Intelligence. It's like when you don't have your glasses on for the day and the world is a little foggy, but once you put those glasses on, everything becomes clear. It's the same with viewing the world through the lens of Emotional Intelligence.

Be excited, feel powerful. They say Superman has x-ray vision, so I want you to walk around with e-ray vision because you understand behavior detection. You've now got all these fancy emotional intelligent skills that have made you a better version of yourself.

Congratulations again; I'm so happy that you have completed this challenge!

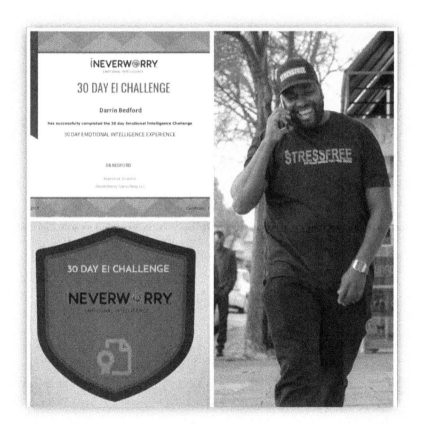

CHALLENGE - DAY 30
FINAL NOTES

About the Author

DB Bedford is a professional Emotional Intelligence consultant and has been consulting and training individuals, organizations, companies and couples for close to 20 years. He has a strong passion for working with youth, families, and the community.

Being an inspiration to others and a role model to his children is of utmost importance. His goal is to leave a legacy behind so that 100 years from now the world will know that he was here.